Part of The Abundance Plan Book Series

THE ABUNDANCE PLAN WORKBOOK
SAVE MONEY AND BUILD WEALTH

www.SaveMoneyandBuildWealth.com

BY KRISTA DUNK AND CHRIS CREEKPAUM

The Abundance Plan Workbook
© 2019 by Krista Dunk and Chris Creekpaum
www.SaveMoneyandBuildWealth.com

This title is also available in Kindle format.

Published by 100X Publishing
Vacaville, CA
www.100Xacademy.com

All rights reserved. No part of this publication may be reproduced, stored in a retrieval system, or transmitted in any form or by any means—for example, electronic, photocopy, recording—without the prior written permission of the publisher.
Scripture taken from the New King James Version®. Copyright © 1982 by Thomas Nelson. Used by permission. All rights reserved.

ISBN: 9-781-6921-4900-0

Printed in the United States of America

This Workbook Belongs to:

_____

Workbook Table of Contents:

How to Use This Workbook	5
What's Your Money Story?	6
The Five Uses of Money	7
Spending Priorities Pyramid Chart	8
Simple Monthly Budget Chart	10
What's Your Next Action Step?	11
Debt Payoff Chart	12
Short-Term and Long-Term Goal Setting	13
Financial Goals Worksheet	14
Examples of Financial Goals	15
Side Hustle Gifts, Abilities and Resources Assessment	16
Investing Ideas	17
Retirement Expense Estimation	18
Grocery Store Meal Planner	19
Bartering Info and Sheet	21
Credit Bureau Sample Letter to Clean Up Your Credit	23
Accounts and Records	26
Notes	27
About the Save Money and Build Wealth Team	30
Speaking and Training	31

How to Use This Workbook

This workbook is a companion resource for Save Money and Build Wealth's Abundance Plan book series. Each section in this workbook corresponds to various ideas and teachings from one of our other books:

Make Your Money Work for You: Level Up Your Finances with New Mindsets, Planning, Habits and Goals

Spiritual Principles of Money

101 Ways to Stretch a Dollar

101 Side Hustles to Make More Money

How to Save Money by DIY'ing Just About Anything

You will find this workbook most helpful after reading our other books or as part of one of our workshops or classes. Feel free to write in this workbook or use a notebook to write answers and information down in. These exercises are meant to get you thinking, planning, organizing and moving towards your money goals.

As a first step in the workbook, take a look at the graphic below. At which level do you feel you are at now, financially? Identifying your current level will help you see what's next on your journey to a new, more successful future with your money.

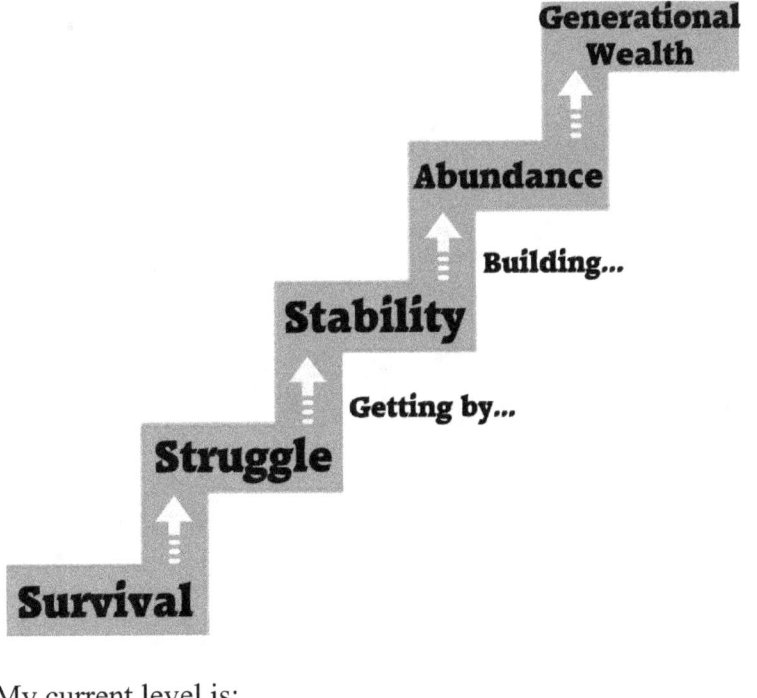

My current level is: _____

What's Your Money Story?

Whether we've ever realized it or not, what we experienced and observed during our childhood years most likely shaped our view of money. Some people grew up with parents who talked about money, and others in families that thought discussing the topic was taboo. Some people got a financial education from their parents, and others only got impressions and perceptions that may or may not have been accurate. What about you?

Growing up, I learned, thought or got the impression money was
_____.

Here are a few ideas as samples to get you thinking:

Unattainable	Scarce
Something to hoard	Attractive
Evil	Was something I wanted a lot of
Something only other people had	Something we just went to the bank for
Something everyone had	Mysterious
Something I should not desire	For giving away
Something we never had enough of	Something I could help others with
Something that made people fight	Something people around me had a lot of
A taboo topic	Something that gave my family status

How would I like to view money now? _____.

THE FIVE USES OF MONEY

This truth comes from Chapter 5 of our Spiritual Principles of Money book. Included here is only a very brief summary to accompany this exercise.

Money has five main uses:

Giving – Saving – Spending – Investing – Enjoying

These five uses can be split into three categories:

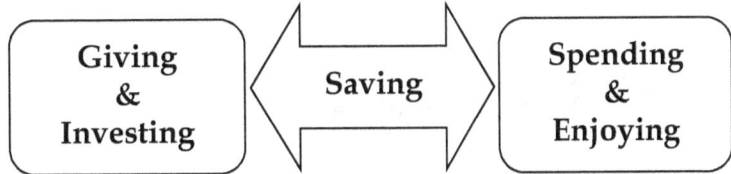

Money is either sown/invested or consumed/spent. Giving and investing are both examples of sowing. When you invest, sow and give, that money is not gone forever. It is growing, and you will see gain and increase come back in the future. Spending and enjoying are examples of how money is consumed. When we spend on necessary needs like utilities, groceries, gas, school fees, rent, that money is gone. The same is true for money we spend on "enjoying." Saving is in a flexible, middle category of its own. It could go either way, e.g., money that is saved could eventually become money that's consumed or be money that's sown.

The wisest use of money is to use it in this order:

1. **Giving** – tithe to a church, charity, help a friend
2. **Saving** – money into a savings account, CD, savings bond, etc.
3. **Spending** – paying bills and necessary expenses
4. **Investing** – putting money into assets and funds
5. **Enjoying** – frills, extras, entertainment, travel, stuff

How are you currently using your money in these categories?

1. Giving – _____
2. Saving – _____
3. Spending – _____
4. Investing – _____
5. Enjoying – _____

SPENDING PRIORITIES PYRAMID:

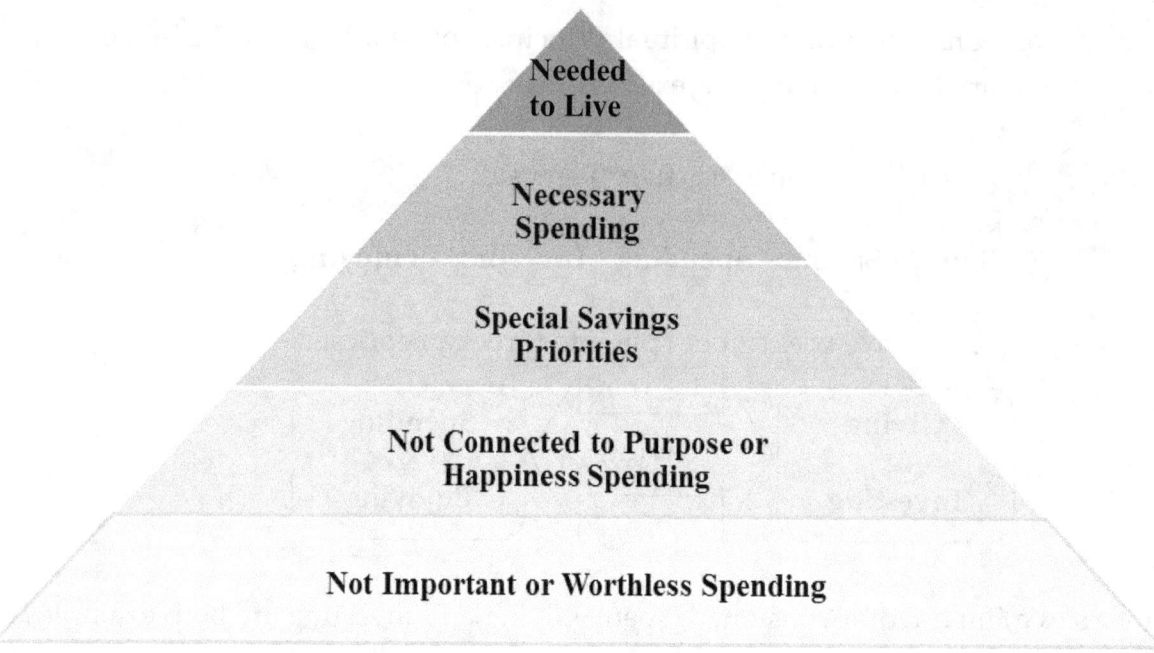

This pyramid chart comes from Chapter 2 in our *Make Your Money Work for You* book.

YOURS TO FILL IN:

We all have expenses in the top *I-need-this-to-live* tier, such as food/water, housing and clothes. *Place your most crucial expenses on the top tier.

Necessary Spending may include things like cell phones, insurance, medical, birthday and holiday gifts, Internet service, car and home maintenance, education costs, and utilities. Not everyone, though, will consider all of these *necessary*. *Identify what your necessary spending items are each month.

Special Savings Priorities will vary for everyone. Some ideas might be travel, investing, education, business equipment, new vehicle, wedding, mission trip, house purchase, medical expense, home improvement project, starting a business, building up an emergency fund, etc. *Discuss and identify what your special savings priority is/priorities are. Your special savings priority should align with your goals.

Things that might be found in the bottom two tiers: school fundraisers, that pair of running shoes (despite not running anymore), pedicures, eating out…again, the as-seen-on-TV gadget, the fancy chrome grill and a muffler kit for a used car, coffee shops, magazines, those pretty earrings, that pretty motorcycle, subscriptions, bars and clubs, get-rich-quick schemes. *Identify items that you spend money on that could be easily eliminated.

Simple Monthly Budget Chart

Month/Year ____/____	
Monthly Income	**Living Expenses**
Pay/salary:	Grocery/Food:
Tips/bonuses:	Eating out:
Investing income:	Entertainment:
Misc. income:	Beauty:
Giving	Clothing:
Tithe:	Healthcare:
Misc:	Childcare:
Saving	Gas:
To savings account:	Subscriptions:
Investing:	Pet care:
Special savings priority:	Insurance:
Vacation:	Vehicle maint./repair:
Misc:	Other:
Housing	**Debt**
Mortgage/Rent:	Vehicle payment:
Taxes/Insurance:	Vehicle payment:
Home services:	Credit card payment:
Repairs/Maintenance:	Credit card payment:
HOA fee:	Credit card payment:
Furniture:	Personal loan payment:
Appliances:	Student loan payment:
Misc:	Other:
Total monthly income:	*Total monthly payments and expenses:*
$	$
Mo. income minus mo. payments/expenses = $	

The last line represents the amount of money remaining per month after all your bills and expenses are paid. If you have a surplus, consider allocating it to your savings, investing or paying down debt (if applicable).

What's Your Next Action Step?

Once an individual or couple has completed and reviewed their budget chart, next steps and plans can be formed. That's when the empowerment starts! Depending on what your budget shows and reveals, your next action steps might be one of these examples:

- ☐ Formulate a Debt Snowball strategy to pay down debt. _____
- ☐ Raise your credit score. _____
- ☐ Figure out a way to bring in more monthly income. _____
- ☐ Determine which expenses could be reduced or eliminated altogether. _____
- ☐ Restructure, consolidate or refinance high interest rate loans. _____
- ☐ Set a dollar amount and save for an emergency fund. _____
- ☐ Set a dollar amount to use/save for investing. _____
- ☐ Plan ahead for known, upcoming expenses. _____
- ☐ Save for a child's college expenses. _____
- ☐ Save for a trip or an upcoming event. _____
- ☐ Make a plan to pay off a home loan. _____
- ☐ Learn about, research and find new ways to grow and invest surplus savings money. _____
- ☐ Invest in CD's, Roth IRA, savings or municipal bonds, money market funds, 401K, etc. _____
- ☐ Invest money into starting a business that generates more cash flow. _____
- ☐ Investments: invest in real estate, agriculture, metals, whole life insurance plans, dividend-paying stocks, land, etc. _____
- ☐ Start looking at/estimating what retirement expenses might be and create retirement income strategies. _____
- ☐ Other: _____ _____

Put a check mark in the box to the left of each item you want to focus on immediately (this month). Our recommendation is to choose one or two (three max) to focus on now. Don't choose too many at one time.

Know there are others you will want to tackle sometime soon? If you know there are other items you want to work on in the near future, write a month or date in on the line provided to the right of each of those.

Debt Payoff Chart

Got loans and other debts? If your next step is to get rid of debt, use this chart to clearly define what they look like now and formulate a strategy to pay them off one by one. Include every debt owed, including home mortgage, vehicles, credit card balances, personal loans, etc.

How to fill out this chart:
Column #1 – Write in the name of each debt and loan, e.g., *house mortgage, Chase Visa, Toyota loan, furniture loan, home equity line of credit (HELOC), loan from Susie*, etc.
Column #2 – Insert each loan or card's monthly payment amount as it is now.
Column #3 – Insert the full balance owed for each debt.
Column #4 – Insert the debt's interest rate.
Columns #5 and #6 – Once you review all your debts, deciding which ones to target for payoff first, second, etc., insert your target payoff dates in column #5 and corresponding payoff priority numbers in column #6. For example, if you plan to payoff a Visa card first because it has the highest interest rate and the second lowest balance owed, write in your goal date for paying it off and put "1" in the priority column. Some people decide to payoff debts with the lowest balance owed first. For most people, a home loan payoff would be ranked last in the priority column.

Once you pay a debt off, congratulations! On to the next! Cross out the whole line and re-work the chart with updated balance due info and priority rankings.

Debt Name	Payment Amt	Balance Owed	Interest Rate	Payoff Goal Date	Priority

Short-Term and Long-Term Goal Setting

Have you heard it said that unwritten goals will almost certainly never materialize? If you think about it, do goals not written down actually exist at all? That's debatable, but if you can take some time to get clear on where it is you want to be in one, two, five, ten, 15, 20 years from now and write it down, you will move towards them. The very act of going through the exercise of contemplating your goals and writing them down increases the probability you will achieve them or at least move in their direction.

SMART:
S – Specific (get as specific as possible)
M – Measurable (milestones, trackable, quantities)
A – Attainable (be sure the goal is realistic and actually achievable)
R – Relevant (this fits into your life and vision, can you do it alone or will you need assistance from others?)
T – Time-Bound (give it a deadline, a target date/timeframe)

SMART goal languaging: I will become proficient in video editing by June 30th and will record, edit and post ten (three to eight minutes long each) promo videos to my business YouTube channel by August 27.

Ineffective goal languaging: I will learn how to video edit and create a YouTube channel.
This is too vague, leaving too many unanswered questions about the goals. When? What kind of videos? How many videos?

As you write out your short-term and long-term goals on the next page, the timeframe is already implied/defined, but keep the other SMART criteria in mind. Specific goals are clear goals. Setting specific goals will help you identify and create habits that support the goals you make.

<u>Self-reflection:</u>
Do I feel apprehensive about setting goals? _____ If so, why?

Financial Goals Worksheet
Twenty-Year Plan for _____

20 Year Goals:
-
-
-

15 Year Goals:
-
-
-

10 Year Goals:
-
-
-

5 Year Goals:
-
-
-

3 Year Goals:
-
-
-

2 Year Goals:
-
-
-

1 Year Goals:
-
-
-

Examples of Financial Goals

Goal Areas:

| Income | Investing | Savings | Debt-Free | Giving | Housing | Education | Events | Insurance |

Income:
Income from regular work/business
Income from assets
Income from multiple streams of income

Investing:
Starting a business
Retirement investments
Real estate
Cash-flow investments
Stock market-based investments
(more ideas during week 6)

Savings:
Emergency fund
Retirement
Save to sow

Giving:
Causes
Missions
Church programs
Charities
Regular tithes/offerings

Housing:
Buying a home
Lease deposits
Investment real estate
Future housing/subsequent houses

Becoming Debt-Free:
Debt snowball
Mortgage payoff

Upcoming Events/Big Purchases:
Wedding
Baby
Travel
Christmas
Car purchase or repair

Education:
Your education
Children's education
Sow into yourself – coaching, training

Legacy, Insurance and Protection:
Adequate Insurance for House/Cars/Life
Will
Trusts

Side Hustle Gifts, Abilities and Resources Assessment

As you consider your options for bringing more money into your budget each month (side hustles), think about what you're good at, education you've received, your natural talents and abilities, plus resources you have at your disposal (things you own).

What skills do you have? What are your abilities? What resources can you put to use? Take a few minutes to write down some ideas. Chris has a few examples below that she's shared with us for some inspiration.

Skills: things you can do/have learned to do because of work experience, special training, practice, acquired knowledge, etc.
<u>My skills include</u>:

Abilities: things that come naturally to you (talents, knowledge, gifts, etc.).
<u>My abilities include</u>:

Resources: things you have access to or a supply available of (i.e., materials, tools, equipment, land, funds, support network of people that could be called upon, etc.) that could be put to use to help you profit.
<u>My resources include</u>:

Chris' Example:

Chris' skills:
Quick reader, crochet, sewing, furniture flipping, crafts, public speaking, learning to be a writer, canning, cooking, Offer Up seller, Ebay seller.

Chris' abilities:
Good with kids and the elderly, organized, resourceful, patient teacher, motivator, love animals.

Chris' resources available:
Truck, trailer, sander, 5 acres of land, apple tree, black berry bushes, canning supplies, riding lawn mower, my mom has a small orchard, my brother is a roofer, my boyfriend is a construction worker, and my daughter is an animal rescuer.

This exercise goes along with our *101 Side Hustles to Make More Money* book.

INVESTING IDEAS

When it comes to investing, there are a lot of options. Not every option is right for every person. They should fit your interests, skill sets, geographic location and personality. Read through this investment idea list and circle the ones that appeal to you.

Owning vacation rental properties	"Opportunity Zone" investment
Rental homes	Land banking
Multi-family investment properties	Collectables (art, coins, cars, historical, etc.)
Property flipping/rehabbing	Loans (you are the bank)
Buying/owning gold, silver or other metals	Accessory Dwelling Unit (ADU)
401K/IRAs	RV storage property and/or rental RV's
Stock Market trading	Diamonds/gemstones/rare jewelry
Options, currency or commodities trading	Offshore investing/banking
Bitcoin/cryptocurrencies	Owing/leasing agricultural/farm property
Invest in/own a business	Aquaponics
Own a franchise	Invest in startup businesses
Oil and gas leases/exploration	Own equipment others want to rent
Buy and hold dividend stocks	Whole Life Insurance

Of the ones you circled, which do you realistically see yourself participating in (or if you already are, plan to continue/do more of) within the next two years?

Five years?

Ten years?

Fifteen years?

Twenty years?

Retirement Expense Estimation

Whether retirement is coming soon for you or is decades away, it's coming and you'll need money! For now, use the categories below to estimate what your monthly expenses may be.

- Housing _____
  Mortgage/Rent _____
  Property taxes _____
  Insurance _____
  Utilities _____
  Maintenance _____
  HOA _____

- Food _____
  Groceries _____
  Dining out _____

- Clothing, home products and personal care items _____

- Medical _____
  Insurance _____
  Medications _____
  Medical services and co-pays _____

- Transportation _____
  Vehicle loan _____
  Gas _____
  Insurance _____
  Public transportation _____
  Vehicle maintenance/repair _____

Debts/Loans _____   Entertainment _____

Travel _____   Gifts _____

Hobbies _____   Charitable contributions _____

Family care _____   Funeral Expenses _____

Estimated total monthly expenses: _____

Bartering Info and Sheet, by Chris the Save Money Maven

Would you like to find or make opportunities to swap, trade and barter? What is bartering?
<u>Barter:</u> to exchange goods or services for other goods or services without using money.

In my local area there is a bartering group found on Facebook. The group has an admin, lists its rules and requires approval to join.

What to look for in a bartering group:
- Are there any Better Business Bureau complaints?
- Number of members
- Length of time in existence
- Reviews by members (past and present)
- Does it comply with IRS rules?
- Is it 100% trade or 50% trade and 50% cash?
- Do people seem to be reasonable in their requests?

Personally, I am very excited to barter and do it often with friends and people I meet. If someone is buying something from me on OfferUp, I always look to see what they're selling and offer a trade with or without cash involved (if there is something they have that I could use). Here are a couple examples of trades I've done recently: my furniture painting services for haircuts and facial waxes and $350 worth of an MLM food company's products just for painting my friend's China hutch. I never would have charged her $350 for painting the hutch, but since she was getting out of that business, she just wanted the stuff gone. My family loves the products, so I eagerly agreed to the trade! I've also sold some of the items that we won't use.

I also love to join "swap" groups; groups like arts and craft items, clothing or jewelry swaps. I've even hosted book swaps! People with young kids often find toy swap groups. Here's how this works: you bring all the items you want to get rid of, you lay out the items on a table or tables, each person draws a number to see who picks first, then second, and so forth. Each person takes one item in turn, until the items are gone or only unwanted items remain. It's fun! I served snacks at the one I hosted! My friends even brought their other friends. It's fun and benefits everyone.

If I was going to start my own bartering group, I would ask each person to fill out a form similar to the one I have created on the next page, then share the summary with everyone in the group. I would look for people who may be interested in my surplus items and ask them if they have any of this or some of that, or would be willing to fix my lawn mower, etc. Sometimes a trade has to involve three people in order to get what you are looking for. Here's an example: you and member #323 trade books for a watch. Member #147 has apples you want and they want the watch. Be sure to communicate all along the way so you aren't stuck with a watch you don't need.

Doesn't this sound fascinating? Keeping more of my hard-earned money and trading things or services with other people is a thrilling idea. We all have stuff we don't need, right? We all can do participate somehow, even if we aren't a professional at it.

Name: _____ Contact info: _____

Abilities: _____
(a God-given talent, something you were born with: singing voice, love kids, good with the elderly, organized, good motivator of people, teacher and training, artist)

Skills: _____
(something you learned by watching or doing: canning, simple haircutting, mediocre cook, scrap booker, stamper, crafter, good at finances, hair styling)

Passions: _____
(something that gets you really excited to do: helping others with big projects, personal finances, sales, flipping furniture, flipping items for a profit, gardening, crafting)

Dislikes: _____
(something you don't want to do: painting houses, snakes, mowing yards ('cuz there are snakes), cigarettes/smoking, medical situations)

Resources: _____
(something you own or have access to: truck with canopy, apple tree, canning equipment, cedar tree, riding mower, sander, tree-cutting equipment, paint sprayer, skill saw, cattle)

Family abilities and resources: _____
(something your family has or can do: salmon fishermen, firewood, grapes, orchard, equipment)

What I need most: _____
(the ideal trade would be for: a house keeper, furniture to flip, car tires, size 2 toddler clothing)

Want: _____
(something you are perpetually looking for: good deals, furniture to paint/change, fresh cut flower bouquets, apples)

Disclaimer: the IRS wants a piece of this pie, so be sure to report your barter as income when filing your taxes.

Grocery Store Meal Planner

When people plan ahead in life, chances are they'll save money! This definitely applies to meal planning. Poor planning in the area of meals can increase the likelihood of two issues: higher cost of food and/or the temptation for unhealthy options. The benefits of planning include saving time, saving money, having a clear plan at the store, and saving your brain space. With a meal planner, there's no more confusion or last-minute scrambling at 4:45 pm, trying to figure out what to do for dinner! Bliss!

We've included a useful meal planner chart already filled in as an example on this page, and a blank one for you to copy and use at your house on the next page.

Day:	**Breakfast**	**Lunch**	**Dinner**	**Snacks**	**Grocery List**
Monday	Waffles, eggs, Sausage, toast	Tuna sandwich, cheese, chips, fruit	Chicken Ceasar salad, lemon, garlic bread	Fruit, raw veggies	Eggs, lemon, garlic bread
Tuesday	Oatmeal, yogurt, fruit	Cold cut sandwiches, apples and peanut butter	Beef barley soup, bread sticks, side salad	fudgsicles	Carrots, barley, yogurt
Wednesday	Egg, ham and cheese sandwiches	Left over barley soup	Spaghetti and meatballs, green beans	Popcorn	Ham, spaghetti sauce, green beans
Thursday	Cold cereal, toast	Cold cuts, oranges, chips	Tater tot casserole with mixed veggies	Grapes	Cream of mushroom soup, grated cheese
Friday	Oatmeal, yogurt, fruit	Tomato soup and cheese sandwiches	Leftovers	Ice cream sundaes	Fudge topping, fresh fruit
Saturday	Cold cereal, toast	Burritos	Grilled pork chops, mashed potatoes, cucumber	Cinnamon rolls	Cucumber, tortillas
Sunday	Potato and sausage casserole	Potato soup and rolls	Yakisoba stir fry	Popcorn, candy	Candy, sausage

Meal Planner for the week of _____

Day:	Breakfast	Lunch	Dinner	Snacks	Grocery List
Monday					
Tuesday					
Wednesday					
Thursday					
Friday					
Saturday					
Sunday					

Credit Bureau Sample Letter to Clean Up Your Credit

Low credit scores can limit your financial options and opportunities in life. It's important to keep current with payments and correct credit report errors if they come up. Request your credit report at least once a year. Read it closely and deal with any inaccuracies immediately. For example, if you do see something that is incomplete, is an inaccurate amount or is not your debt at all, you will need to write a letter to the three main credit bureaus and dispute the item.

There are three credit bureaus in the United States that keep track of payment history and your financial data. Here they are:

Equifax
P.O. Box 740256
Atlanta, GA 30374

TransUnion LLC Consumer Dispute Center
P.O. Box 2000
Chester, PA 19016

Experian Dispute
P.O. Box 4500
Allen, TX 75013

On the next page, there is a sample letter with specific wording you can use. Type it up, make three copies, sign and date them, attach all corresponding materials and documentation regarding this debt, and mail them off immediately to all three credit bureaus.

Your name and return address
Date

Dear Sirs:

I am writing this letter in response to the phone call/letter received from you on (Date). In conformance to my rights under the Fair Debt Collection Practices Act (FDCPA), I am requesting you to provide me with a validation of the debt that you talked of earlier. Please note, this is not a refusal to pay, rather a statement that your claim is disputed and validation is demanded. (15 USC 1692g Sec. 809 (b))

I do hereby request that your office provide me with complete documentation to verify that I owe the said debt and have any legal obligation to pay you.

Please provide me with the following:
- Agreement with the creditor that authorizes you to collect on this alleged debt
- The agreement bearing my signature stating that I have agreed to assume the debt
- Valid copies of the debt agreement stating the amount of the debt and interest charges
- Proof that the Statute of Limitations has not expired
- Complete payment history on this account along with an accounting of all additional charges being assessed
- Show me that you are licensed to collect in my state; and
- Your license numbers and Registered Agent

If your office fails to reply to this debt validation letter within 30 days from the date of your receipt, all instances related to this account must be immediately deleted and completely removed from my credit file. Moreover, all future attempts to collect on the said debt must be ceased.

Your non-compliance with my request will also be construed as an absolute waiver of all claims to enforce the debt against me and your implied agreement to compensate me for court costs and attorney fees if I am forced to bring this matter before a judge.

Thank you,

Your Signature   Date
Your Printed Name

Credit Bureau and Credit Score Topic Continued:

Once you've sent off your letters, the credit bureaus will investigate your dispute. They only have 30 days to verify the account is yours or it must be deleted from your report. Also, they cannot charge you for this service. Medical debt is one of the easiest types of debt to get removed because of the HIPPA privacy laws. If the item is not removed from your credit report, don't give up. Try the process again in a couple of months.

If you still aren't successful and the debt is yours, ask for a "pay for delete." In this case, you will be negotiating a payment with the collection agency, the store, hospital, etc., directly, and then the credit bureau will delete the collection account from your credit report. Sometimes you can negotiate what you own down by 40% of the original debt amount. Just be sure to get this payoff agreement in writing from them before you make the payment.

If it's still not removed from your credit report after this "pay for delete" process, you will need to re-dispute the charge with the credit bureaus. You will now be able to go back to the credit bureau and dispute the item again and hope the creditor does not go through the hassle of validating a debt that's been paid. They have no incentive to do it, so they may not respond to the credit bureau's request.

If it still shows up, wait for the account to be sold to another agency and dispute it again. Debt is constantly being sold and re-sold from collection agency to collection agency. At this point the creditor listed on your credit report no longer has your account information, so you can dispute it and may finally have luck having it deleted.

Accounts and Records

An accountant friend of mine once told me a story of a woman newly widowed who knew ZERO about her finances, because her late husband took care of everything. She didn't pay attention to account numbers or balances, debts owed, insurance or investment accounts...zip. When he passed away, she was left wondering what to do. We've created this short document in order for you to keep track of important assets, account numbers or anything else someone would need to know about in case of emergency (and for your own tracking purposes). Because this page may have sensitive, confidential information on it, you may want to keep this book in a financial file, tucked away or make a copy of this page to fill out and have it filed away separately.

Add contact info, account numbers, addresses, phone numbers, passwords, or other important details. This info is current as of (month/year): _____ / _____.

Checking Account Info: _____
_____
_____

Savings Account Info: _____
_____
_____

Medical Insurance Account Info: _____
_____
_____

Life Insurance Company: _____
_____
_____

401K/IRA Info: _____
_____

Mortgage and Homeowner's Insurance Details: _____
_____
_____

Property Tax Info: _____
_____

Utility Accounts: _____
_____
_____

Notes

Notes

Notes

About the Save Money and Build Wealth Team

Chris Dunk, Krista Dunk and Chris Creekpaum

At Save Money and Build Wealth, the goal is teaching for transformation, not just information. There's plenty of financial information out there, but sometimes people need a fresh perspective, practical ideas, someone they can relate to and/or individualized help. We understand!

Chris, the Save-Money Maven, Creekpaum is masterful at all things thrifty. She has been helping friends, neighbors, relatives and co-workers for years with credit repair, DIY classes, finding deals, how to be resourceful, and giving sound money advice. Chris has a huge heart to see people up-level their financial status and find creative ideas to stretch every dollar they have and to make more money. By day, Chris has a "real job" working for state government, and she also has several online businesses. She has been a single mother for the past 18 years, and in that time has put her herself and her daughter, Kayla, through college, both receiving their bachelor's degrees with almost no student loans.

Chris, the Make-Money Master, and Krista, the Money-Mindset Maven, Dunk have had many money-related experiences over the course of their 26+-year marriage. Their goal is to help people avoid financial pitfalls (some of which they fell into themselves…) and to get a new vision for how their lives could look when new mindsets and habits are put into practice. Going from small beginnings and debt, they are now in a place of financial peace and abundance and want to see others do the same. Chris works in the IT industry for an international company, and Krista manages their investments and is the project director for two book publishing companies. Because of their passion for teaching and their love of financial strategy, they have been called "an idea factory." Chris and Krista have two teenagers and enjoy serving in their local church.

Learn more about who we are and what we do at **www.SaveMoneyandBuildWealth.com**. Also join us in our Facebook group at **www.facebook.com/groups/savemoneyandbuildwealth.**

We look forward to meeting you!
Chris, Krista and Chris

Speaking and Training

Interested in speakers for your group, event, conference, church, or online training on faith and finance topics? Looking to host a special workshop or need small group curriculum to help people save money and build wealth?

Connect with the Save Money and Build Wealth team today – Chris, Krista and Chris! This power trio is fun, experienced and loves to help others get breakthrough in the area of money and finances. They are also dedicated to helping people get new, biblically-based mindsets that will give them freedom in many areas of their lives.

Money-Related Training Topic Examples:

101 Ways to Make More Money	Teen and Young Adult Money Success Kickstart
101 Ways to Stretch a Dollar	Stewarding Money God's Way
The 5 Uses of Money	Money Mindset for Abundance
Financial Goal Setting	Discovering Your Money Journey's Next Step

Connect with our team today at **TheAbundancePlan@gmail.com**
or on our Facebook group page at **www.facebook.com/groups/savemoneyandbuildwealth**

The Abundance Plan Book Series:
Available Now:

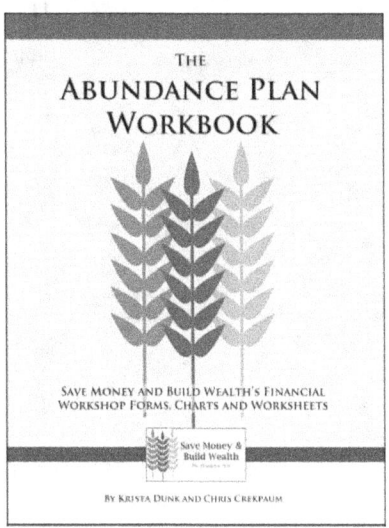

Coming soon:
Save Money by DIY'ing Just About Anything
101 Ways to Stretch a Dollar
101 Side Hustles to Make More Money

Save Money and Build Wealth resources are proudly published by:

Exclusive Publishing for Kingdom Entrepreneurs
www.100Xacademy.com

www.ingramcontent.com/pod-product-compliance
Lightning Source LLC
Chambersburg PA
CBHW081708220526
45466CB00009B/2917